Wealth-Building through Gaming

Capitalizing on eSports Opportunities

Table of Contents

Chapter 1. Introduction

Dive into the dynamic and exhilarating world of eSports in our Special Report: "Wealth-Building through Gaming: Capitalizing on eSports Opportunities". This engaging document peels back the layers of this fast-growing industry and presents a novel approach to wealth-building that is not only eye-opening but potentially lucrative. No longer is gaming the domain of leisure alone; it has evolved into a bona fide investment opportunity, commanding serious attention from mainstream investors. Our report decodes the complexities of this adrenaline-fueled sector, showing you how to capitalize on its meteoric rise. Whether you're a gaming enthusiast willing to turn your passion into profit, or an investor hunting for the next big thing, this special report makes the compelling case that eSports might just be your trophy. Experience the thrill of eSports and unlock your financial potential, all in one captivating read!

Chapter 2. Understanding the eSports Landscape

It is critically important to first understand the origin and evolution of eSports. Standing for electronic sports, eSports simply refers to competitive video gaming at a professional level. The competitive element sets it apart from casual gaming, with structured matches and tournaments involving professional players and teams.

From their inception in the late 1970s and early 1980s, video games have come a long way. Driven by advances in computing power, graphics, player interfaces, internet technology, and game design, they have transformed from minor diversions into a powerful, multifaceted type of entertainment.

2.1. The Birth of eSports

eSports as a concept began to take shape in the 1970s with the advent of the first multiplayer games. However, the noticeable inception of international eSports competitions did not occur until 1980 with the Space Invaders Championship, held by Atari, which drew over 10,000 participants across the US.

As internet connectivity improved and became more widespread during the late 90s and early 2000s, eSports began to bloom, enabled by the proliferation of competitive games, online leagues, and tournaments. Pioneering eSports titles during this era, such as Quake, Counter-Strike, and StarCraft, amassed large, dedicated player bases.

2.2. The Rise of Modern eSports

With the introduction of streaming platforms like Twitch in 2011, eSports reached a new height — it became a spectator sport.

Attracting millions of viewers globally, eSports transitioned from a niche culture to mainstream entertainment.

Today, eSports is a rapidly growing industry, with top professional gamers and teams competing in tournaments with million-dollar prize pools, sometimes even surpassing traditional sports events. Some of the most iconic title includes Dota 2, League of Legends, Fortnite, and Counter-Strike: Global Offensive.

2.3. eSports as an Industry

Although professional competitions are the most visible aspect of eSports, they are just one element of a growing industry. eSports encompasses game development, player management, event hosting, broadcasting, marketing, and software or hardware development, all of which overlap with other areas of the larger gaming industry.

eSports also includes ancillary markets such as online betting and fantasy leagues. Furthermore, the rise of mobile eSports is making competitive gaming more accessible, particularly in regions such as Asia and South America, where mobile technology dominates.

2.4. Major Industry Stakeholders

Examining the eSports ecosystem involves understanding its various stakeholders, who play significant roles in shaping this industry.

1. **Game Publishers and Developers:** Companies like Riot Games, Valve Corporation, Activision Blizzard, and Epic Games develop popular eSports titles. These organizations usually organize their own tournaments, shaping the eSports landscape in the process.

2. **Teams and Players:** eSports teams and players are akin to traditional sports teams and athletes. They participate in tournaments, have fan followings, and endorse brands. Top teams operate on a global scale and are often associated with

major brand sponsorships.

3. **Broadcasting Platforms:** Streaming platforms like Twitch, YouTube Gaming, and Mixer have brought eSports into people's homes, desktops, and mobile devices, connecting gamers and fans like never before.

4. **Event Organizers:** Companies specializing in organizing eSports events play a key role in maintaining the spectacle. They coordinate games, manage venues, and (in non-pandemic times) handle live audiences.

5. **Sponsors and Advertisers:** The eSports industry attracts significant investments from sponsors and advertisers, often from outside the gaming industry. They provide the money required to host tournaments, pay athletes, and support teams.

2.5. Financial Aspects of eSports

Investments and profits in esports come from various sources, including advertising, sponsorship, media rights, team franchising, and tournament winnings. In 2020, reports estimated global eSports revenues to reach $1.1 billion, with $822.4 million (75%) coming from media rights and sponsorship.

2.6. The Future of eSports

As eSports continues to mature as an industry, we can expect the arrival of more sophisticated business and revenue models. New trends suggest the growth potential of eSports in education, with more universities offering eSports programs, scholarships, and even courses in related disciplines.

In sum, the eSports landscape is a rich and vibrant one, with steady progression, wide-ranging implications, and vast entrepreneurial potential. With the right knowledge, strategy, and investment, stakeholders can find profitable opportunities in this dynamic realm.

Chapter 3. The Financial Evolution of Gaming

The shift in perspective towards gaming as a predominantly recreational hobby to a legitimate source of income sprouted upon the advent of eSports and the video game streaming phenomenon. In the nascent days of gaming, sources of income were limited to the creation and sales of games themselves. However, the landscape has swiftly changed, leaving an indelible impression on the global economy, entailing an intricate discussion.

3.1. The Monetization of Gaming

In the early years of video gaming, the primary market was catered to by a limited range of game developers and consoles. As technology became more advanced, barriers to entry decreased as did the cost of production, thus leading to a higher number of gaming companies vying for a slice of the market. With an influx of competition, monetization strategies began to diverge from simple box copy sales to various innovative revenue models.

In-game purchases, subscription services, and premium versions became industry standards as a reliable source of continuous revenue. More recently, incorporating advertising within games, especially in mobile gaming, opened up new avenues for wealth generation. Strategic partnerships and sponsorships are also forming a sizeable fraction of gaming companies' revenue streams.

3.2. The Rise of eSports

The inception of eSports remarkably reshaped the financial versatility of the gaming industry. Players were no longer isolated to a solitary experience but could compete against others at a professional level, bringing about a rise in competitive gaming. Tournaments became the nucleus of this trend, offering lucrative prize pools that could rival traditional sports. Industry giants like Dota 2, Fortnite and League of Legends host championships with multi-million dollar prizes, greatly changing the economic dynamics of gaming.

In addition, these tournaments' mass appeal has led to a boom in eSports broadcasting, both through traditional channels and the pioneers of streaming platforms like Twitch and YouTube Gaming. These lucrative broadcasting rights are another high income stream in this industry.

3.3. The Economic Value of Game Streaming

Broadcasting live gameplay became a phenomenon that amplified the connection between gamers and audiences. It ballooned beyond hobbyists uploading gameplay videos to a full-fledged profession backed by powerful companies. Major players such as Microsoft, Amazon, Google, and Facebook are pumping in vast sums of money to capitalize on this trend.

Streamer revenue is multi-faceted combining donations and subscription fees from viewers, partnership deals with streaming platforms, sponsorships from various industries, and revenue from merchandise and advertising. The result is enhanced income potential for streamers, codifying game streaming as a viable career choice.

Famous streamers create high engagement, influencing game sales and in-game trends, distorting the financial impact on the gaming market. The Twitch platform has redefined audience expectations and shone light on a fresh monetization method in viewer donations, a substantial income stream.

3.4. Investment in the Gaming Industry

With the dichotomy between entertainment and investment becoming blurred, the gaming world offers unique opportunities for investors. The principal way investors tap into the gaming market's profits is by buying shares of publicly traded game development studios, streaming platforms, or hardware manufacturers.

An emerging trend is seen in the rise of ETFs (Exchange Traded Funds) focused on the gaming sector, offering diversified exposure to this rapidly growing market. Risk and return profile changes drastically compared to investing in individual companies, highlighting the need for diligent analysis to balance potential gains versus volatility.

Venture capitalists are also very active in gaming, particularly in esports and streaming platforms' nascent stages, where they see significant potential. In-game advertising and partnerships with businesses are now becoming major areas for investment.

3.5. The Potential of Cryptocurrency and Blockchain

Innovation is in the DNA of the gaming industry. The potential of integrating new technologies such as cryptocurrency and blockchain is being tentatively explored. Blockchain could drastically reduce piracy and provide better security.

Games such as CryptoKitties and Decentraland suggest that cryptocurrencies could be used to purchase in-game items, providing a tangible value to these digital assets, thus creating a completely new wealth stream for gamers and investors alike.

In summary, the financial evolution of gaming has traversed a fascinating journey, from being a niche market to becoming a mainstream powerhouse. A unique combination of technology, cultural acceptance, and innovation has contributed to this financial revolution. Its continued potential for wealth creation and financial growth makes it a compelling opportunity for avid gamers, prospective professionals, and astute investors. The future of the gaming industry indeed promises to be lucrative and thrilling.

Chapter 4. Players, Teams, and Tournaments: The Building Blocks of eSports

The eSports industry functions somewhat similarly to traditional sports, with leagues, teams, and tournaments serving as the mainstay. However, it's not just the sporting events themselves that matter, but also the players and teams who perform in them, and the wider ecosystem.

In this section, we will delve into how the nature of eSports, players, and teams reflects and impacts this exciting financial medium's potential.

4.1. The Power of Players

In eSports, individual players drive fans' interests and engagement, similar to how athletes command the sporting world. They dare not only for the honor of victory but also for lucrative monetary rewards that might set any financial analyst's heart racing.

In the early 2000s, eSports players were generally unrecognized and undervalued. At best, they were viewed as hobbyists; at worst, they were stigmatized. However, times have changed. Some of the best players command six-figure salaries now, excluding win bonuses and endorsement deals. The inclusion of eSports in the Asian Games and potentially in the Olympics highlights the global recognition these players now receive.

Besides their competitive earnings, another factor affecting a player's wealth-building capabilities is their digital following. Players who master the art of self-branding—by live streaming their gameplay and building a loyal fanbase—create additional income streams through advertising, sponsorship, and merchandise.

4.2. The Essence of Teams

Teams are integral to eSports, mirroring their importance in traditional sports. eSports teams involve an amalgamation of individual players, coaches, managers, and support staff, not very dissimilar to traditional sports squads.

The eSports teams not only participate in tournaments but also manage player contracts and development, seek sponsorships, sell merchandise, and engage with fans. More recently, an increasing number of teams have begun investing in training facilities, reflecting financial success and commitment to competitive advantage and player welfare.

In terms of investment prospects, eSports teams are attractive targets. Shopify's CEO, for instance, has invested in an eSports team. The allure comes from multiple income streams—from tournament winnings, player transfers, sponsorships, advertising, broadcasting rights, and merchandise sales—each with the potential to yield substantial returns.

4.3. The Tournament Terrain

Tournaments are the beating heart of the eSports ecosystem. They provide the platform where players and teams battle it out, often in front of millions of viewers worldwide. From the early days of LAN parties to today's multimillion-dollar competitions in packed arenas, eSports tournaments have come a long way.

Tournaments are typically funded through sponsorships, ticket sales, and broadcast rights. The prize pools have been ballooning with each passing year. For instance, The Dota 2 International 2019 saw a prize pool of over $34 million, far outstripping many traditional sporting events.

Major tournaments also stimulate activity in related industries, such as hospitality, broadcast media, marketing, and tourism. For investors, this presents an additional set of opportunities beyond the gaming industry itself.

4.4. The Network Effect: Fans, Online Platforms, and Sponsors

While not directly part of the player-team-tournament trifecta, fans and followers, online platforms, and sponsors form the broader ecosystem that supports and enhances the value of these entities.

Fans are primarily responsible for the sector's explosive growth, providing both a market for products and a source of revenue through advertising, subscriptions, donations, and more. The speed and ease with which eSports can be broadcasted globally via online platforms have allowed for a highly engaged, global fan base. With over 495 million fans in 2020 and growing year on year, the market is certainly promising.

Online streaming platforms like Twitch and YouTube have opened the door to a more engaged fan experience. Moreover, the symbiotic relationship between platforms and players amplifies wealth creation opportunities for both entities.

Finally, sponsors are the lifeblood of the eSports economy. Driven by the growing fan base, household names like Intel, Coca Cola, Mercedes, and more have entered the eSports sponsorship scene, infusing more money into the ecosystem and enhancing the financial prospects.

4.5. Outlook and Opportunities

The eSports landscape – from players to teams and tournaments – provides a fertile ground for wealth building. As we unpacked the features and analyzed the financial aspects of these building blocks, it's clear that eSports hold a unique investment potential.

With its all-digital nature, eSports has transcended many limitations of traditional sports industries. It has an impressive reach, opening up multiple revenue streams for participants and investors alike. If you're looking for a novel and potentially lucrative investment avenue, eSports might well be the trophy you're hunting for.

Monitor the eSports landscape, keep an eye on the rising teams and players, and be open to opportunities that align with the growth trajectories within this fast-paced universe! The game is on, and the ball is in your court.

Chapter 5. The Revenue Streams of eSports: Beyond the Game

The foundation of the eSports industry is without a doubt the captivating games themselves. However, while the competition unfolds on the screens of millions of spectators worldwide, there's much more contributing to the flourishing revenue of the sector. Comprehensive exploration of these revenue streams can offer individual investors and corporations alike a safe passage into the wealth-building opportunities presented by this booming industry.

5.1. Prize Money and Player Salaries

Prize money can reach astronomical heights in famous eSports events. For instance, the prize pool for The International Dota 2 Championships in 2019 surpassed $34 million, outpacing the reward offered at many traditional sports championships. However, by the general rule, prize money is not a reliable income stream for teams or individuals. The winnings are primarily reserved for tier-one players and are highly unpredictable, swayed by ever-changing team dynamics and performance factors.

Bringing in regular income are the player salaries, which has also witnessed a solid upward trend as the industry matures. With the stabilizing salaried contracts, eSports athletes are supported monetarily while they hone their skills for high-stakes competitions.

5.2. Sponsorships

Sponsorships unfold as one of the most viable financial backbones of the competitive gaming industry. Brands, both endemic and non-endemic to the gaming industry, take advantage of the vast, engaged audience to sell their products and services. This symbiotic relationship allows companies to harness the power of influencer marketing while simultaneously supporting the eSports industry.

Sponsors generally provide funds in exchange for advertisement opportunities like brand placements or personal endorsements. Endemic sponsors, such as Intel or Razer, are companies offering gaming hardware, software, or related services. Non-endemic sponsors, such as Coca-Cola or Mercedes-Benz, see value in the rapidly growing and youthful eSports demographic.

5.3. Broadcasting Rights and Streaming

As eSports popularity continues to skyrocket, broadcasting rights are being bought and sold for increasingly high sums. Major platforms like Amazon-owned Twitch, YouTube Gaming, and China's Huya spend hefty amounts to ensure exclusive rights to stream popular eSports events.

These platforms generate income through advertising, donations, and subscription fees. They also allow individual players and teams to earn money through brand partnerships and fan donations. More recently, media behemoth ESPN has ventured into televising eSports, serving as further testament to the growth of the sector.

5.4. Merchandising and Licensing

The world of eSports has given birth to a thriving market of team merchandise. From event-specific paraphernalia to general team apparel, fans worldwide enthusiastically purchase merchandise to support their favorite teams. Similar to traditional sportswear, eSports' merchandise includes jerseys, caps, scarves, as well as digital goods like in-game skins and emotes.

A related source of revenue comes from the licensing of video game content. Game developers often sell the rights to their content for use in broadcasts and other merchandising endeavors. Such practices are mutually beneficial, boasting the game's popularity while bringing it additional earnings.

5.5. Betting and Fantasy eSports

Just like traditional sports, betting has found its way into eSports. The competitive nature, coupled with an engaged audience, makes eSports an appealing prospect for online betting companies. As a result, betting has grown into a lucrative segment of the eSports economy. In tandem, fantasy eSports platforms, where players create and bet on 'fantasy teams', have also gained significant popularity.

While these revenue streams are contributing to the tremendous growth of the eSports industry, they also bring forth opportunities for savvy investors. As gaming continues to evolve and solidify its place in mainstream entertainment, profit avenues within the sector are proliferating. Hence, a well-aimed investment in eSports presents more potential than ever to culminate into handsome returns. Essentially, the game's vibrant world extends far beyond the competition; it's a new domain of innovative business models and wealth-building possibilities.

Chapter 6. eSports and Digital Media: The New Frontiers

Note: Due to text limitations, a complete 5-page A4 document cannot be generated in one response. Here is a substantial portion for the requested chapter.

In the thrilling, fast-paced realm of eSports, the synergy between digital media and competitive gaming elevates the industry's potential for growth, consolidation and maturation. This symbiosis ensures that eSports remains at the center of the digital revolution, blurring the boundaries between interactive entertainment and spectator sport.

6.1. The Rising Tide of eSports

The emergence of eSports is a vivid demonstration of how digitization can revolutionize an industry. Driving this trend is a youth-driven culture that thrives on the thrill and camaraderie of engaging in competitive digital entertainment. The effect of eSports on shaping modern entertainment consumption habits cannot be ignored.

Competitive electronic gaming, or eSports, has been on a relentless rise. From a niche hobby for video game enthusiasts, eSports has become a booming sector with millions of followers worldwide and billions of dollars circulating annually, as per Newzoo's Global eSports Market Report. The large arenas, once exclusively the domain of traditional physical sports, are now regularly occupied by eSports tournaments garnering vast audiences.

Online streaming platforms like Twitch, YouTube Gaming, and

Facebook Gaming are at the heart of this growth by providing an exciting and accessible avenue for spectators to watch their favorite eSport athletes compete, and for those competitors to earn significant income through advertisements, partnerships, and fan donations.

6.2. Digital Media - The Catalyst

Digital media plays a central role in propelling eSports to mainstream consciousness. For an industry where the competition happens within the confines of virtual games, the role of digital media to project the spectacle to audiences cannot be overstated.

Digital platforms, from social networks to dedicated gaming channels, drive the lion's share of eSports content distribution. The emergence of live-streaming and on-demand video platforms has enabled a vast number of enthusiasts to become creators themselves, leading to an explosion in player-created content. This has fostered a vibrant community within the global eSports audience that thrives on a steady diet of game walkthroughs, highlight compileties, and personality-driven commentary.

Broadband connectivity, more affordable and powerful gaming rigs, and advancements in video game design have also been cornerstones in cementing eSports' foothold in the mainstream sporting landscape. The transition to interactive, immersive, and competitive experiences from the passive consumption of traditional media is further fueling the sector's growth.

6.3. The Role of Social Networks

Social networks have become instrumental in promoting the growth of eSports and gaming-like experiences. In this symbiotic relationship, digital platforms essentially act as multiplier effects for eSports in terms of expanding its reach, heightening engagement, and adding revenue streams.

Talking about social media and gaming in the same breath, it would be inappropriate not to mention Twitch. The Twitch platform, designed to bring gaming enthusiasts together, demonstrates just how eSports and social media can merge for mutual benefit. Gamers livestream their gaming sessions, talk with viewers and fans, promote their personal brands, collaborate with other streamers, and earn money from sponsorships and fan donations.

YouTube Gaming is another platform leveraging community-centric features to engage gaming fans. Facebook Gaming, despite trailing behind Twitch and YouTube in terms of viewership, gives streamers access to monetization tools and broadens audiences by integrating into Facebook's expansive ecosystem.

6.4. The Finances of Digital and eSports

The eSports industry's successful interaction with digital media has paved the way for several revenue streams to develop, adding heft to its financial profile. The primary revenue drivers include media rights, streaming content, sponsorships and advertising, merchandise sales, and game publisher fees.

With the surge in eSports' popularity, many traditional media companies are also diving into this market. The battle for media rights to high-demand eSports events mirrors that experienced in traditional sports, with content distributors willing to secure streaming rights for eSports tournaments and leagues.

Collaboration with brands for sponsorship and advertising is another major factor contributing to eSports revenue. Brands, keen to reach out to the millennial and Gen Z demographics, are increasingly investing in eSports through various partnerships and endorsements. This development advances the argument for considering eSports as a legitimate investment opportunity.

This was just an overview of the complex and dynamic interaction between eSports and digital media. As competitive gaming continues its upward trajectory, it is essential to stay abreast of the industry trends and understand how they factor into the profitability and feasibility of eSports investments.

To be continued...

Chapter 7. Investing in eSports Stocks: A Primer

Investing in eSports isn't some abstract concept; it's a tangible, executable strategy with immense potential. However, the approach requires due diligence, a robust understanding of the industry, and frequent monitoring as it's an emerging niche within the broader tech-agglomerate. That said, eSports is quickly becoming a fertile ground for potential investors.

7.1. Recognizing the Momentum

As an investor, the first step is to recognize the relevance and momentum the eSports industry has been gathering. Many investors tend to overlook eSports as a minor offshoot of the larger gaming industry, but the reality is much more exciting. eSports is an industry propelled by its stand-alone momentum, and it's gaining recognition in mainstream media and the capital market. Investment in eSports-related companies has surged over the past years, indicating the industry's growth and potential.

7.2. Dissecting the Market

The eSports industry is multifaceted with various verticals to consider. Primarily, you have game developers, teams, leagues, streaming platforms, and hardware manufacturers. To make sound investment decisions, it's important to understand these entities' individual roles and their interconnectedness.

For example, game developers such as Activision Blizzard, Electronic Arts, and Tencent are popular investment picks because their games form the backbone of eSports.

Streaming platforms like Amazon-owned Twitch and Google's YouTube are vital too as they broadcast tournaments to millions around the globe.

Similarly, eSports specific organizations like Gfinity and Super League Gaming provide infrastructure for professional eSports competitions.

7.3. Analysing eSports Stocks

ESports stocks, like any other stocks, require careful analysis before you dive in. Familiarize yourself with traditional tools of financial analysis such as Price/Earnings (P/E) ratios, earnings yield, debt-to-equity ratio, and sector-specific metrics. Also, keeping an eye on the competitive landscape within the industry can prove beneficial.

For instance, if one company secures exclusive broadcasting rights for a popular tournament, it may mean an increase in revenue and thus influencing the stock positively.

Keep in mind that while many eSports organizations are privately held, there's still a range of publicly traded companies directly linked to the industry, be it through game development, broadcasting, or hardware manufacturing.

7.4. Investing through ETFs

Another way to capitalize on the eSports industry without having to analyze individual stocks is through Exchange Traded Funds (ETFs). ETFs like the VanEck Vectors Video Gaming and eSports ETF (ESPO) or Global X Video Games & Esports ETF (HERO) provide investors exposure to a portfolio of businesses invested in video gaming and eSports.

Generally, ETFs, because of their inherent diversification, help reduce the risk associated with investing in a single stock. They are ideal for investors who believe in the sector's promise but aren't comfortable putting their eggs in one basket.

7.5. Watching Trends

Lastly, regular tracking of the eSports industry's trends can help you make better investment decisions. Key trends include:

- Emergence of new games: New games can rapidly ascend in popularity, driving significant revenue for the game's developers and related ecosystem.

- Market penetration in new regions: As the industry expands into new territories, companies that establish early presences may find themselves well-positioned for growth.

- Technological advancements: Hardware makers providing equipment (like VR headsets) and software providers offering services (like cloud gaming platforms) will likely benefit from technological advancements.

- Regulatory developments: Any changes to regulations around things like gambling, broadcasting rights, and licensing could have a significant impact on eSports companies.

Ultimately, an in-depth understanding of these facets will allow you to invest wisely in eSports stocks. Embracing the 'players' of this exhilarating digital arena could lead you to prosperous returns and an enthralling investment journey. Just remember that as with all investments, eSports investing entails risk, and it's crucial to invest responsibly and keep your financial goals front and center.

Chapter 8. Sponsorships and Partnerships: The Big Game Plan

The global eSports market, largely powered by brand sponsorships and partnerships, has experienced unprecedented growth. This accelerating evolution of the eSports landscape has offered unique opportunities for brands, sponsorships, partnerships, and monetization, as we will see in the following sections.

8.1. The Evolution of Sponsorships and Partnerships

eSports began in the early 2000s as a niche competitor to traditional sports. Over the years, an evolution in this sphere has ushered in a plethora of sponsorships and partnerships. Traditional sports brands were some of the earliest partners for eSports tournaments and professional teams, viewing it as a strategic move to engage a young, tech-savvy audience.

Advancements in technology and the rise in popularity of live-streaming platforms, such as Twitch, led to a surge in the viewership of eSports. Companies started to notice the value of reaching this vast pool of engaged users, opening the floodgates for non-endemic brand sponsorships.

8.2. Impact of Non-Endemic Brands

Non-endemic brands, those outside gaming and technology sectors such as fast-food chains, beverage companies, and automobile manufacturers, have found the eSports market too valuable to overlook. Moreover, these sponsorships and partnerships have proved instrumental in adding legitimacy to the eSports domain.

Such brands collaborate on a multitude of integration levels within the eSports world - right from presenting major tournaments to establishing long-term partnerships with professional eSports teams.

8.3. Key Partnerships: A Glimpse into the Success Stories

High profile collaborations mark the continually evolving eSports sponsorship scene. For instance, the partnership between BMW and five major eSports clubs, Mercedes-Benz's partnership with the League of Legends World Championship, and Coca-Cola's alliances with the Overwatch League and various eSports teams highlight the massive potential held by this sector.

These partnerships extend beyond the realm of simple sponsorship contracts. Brands invest in eSports stadiums, team training facilities, enhancing prize pools, and player welfare - contributing to the growth and development of the industry.

8.4. Tapping into the eSports Audiences: A Marketing Goldmine

The eSports audience, being distinct, tech-savvy, and highly engaged, offers a unique marketing opportunity for brands. Enthusiastic and loyal, these viewers invest significant time and resources into supporting their favorite teams and games.

Marketers continually push their boundaries for a unique, immersive, and interactive approach through in-game advertising, real-life activations, and merchandise to tap into this lucrative audience.

8.5. Achieving Effective Brand Integration in eSports

It's not merely about being present in the eSports environment, but how well a brand can integrate itself that determines its success. The most successful partnerships occur when a brand can incorporate its product or service in a way that enhances the audience's eSports experience, such as employing AI technology for game analytics or VR for immersive viewing experiences.

8.6. Challenges Ahead: Addressing the Hurdles

Despite the myriad advantages, the challenges of achieving successful brand integration in eSports should not be downplayed. Understanding the eSports audience, establishing effective communication, and dealing with the rapidly changing nature of games, leagues, and players are just a few issues to consider.

In conclusion, sponsorships and partnerships are instrumental in the eSports arena. Achieving effective brand integration in eSports requires navigating challenges while capitalizing on opportunities. Brands drawn to the wide, vibrant eSports landscape have unveiled innovative approaches to connect with audiences, transforming the gaming arena into a marketplace. The dynamic eSports environment continues to push limits, serving as an exciting hotbed for growth and investment.

Chapter 9. Exploring eSports Betting and Fantasy Leagues

ESports betting can be seen as one of the most significant growth industries within the entire global betting sphere. Just a decade ago, it was virtually non-existent. Today, in the mid and late 2020s, we're seeing multimillion-dollar prize pools, extensive betting options, and hundreds of thousands – if not millions – of passionate spectators and bettors.

9.1. The Basics of eSports

To understand betting related to eSports, one first needs to understand what eSports actually is. Simply put, eSports stands for Electronic Sports, encompassing games played competitively at a high level. These games can range from first-person shooters (FPS) like Counter-Strike: Global Offensive, to Multiplayer Online Battle Arena (MOBA) games like League of Legends or DOTA 2.

These games are organized into tournaments where professional teams compete for prize pools that often run up to millions of dollars. The tournaments are usually held in large arenas, often filled to the brim with passionate fans, with millions more tuning in online via streaming services like Twitch or YouTube.

ESports' allure is in its entertaining gameplay and the high level of skill exhibited by professional players, making it as much a spectator sport as traditional sports. This dynamic has laid the foundation for a booming betting industry surrounding eSports.

9.2. Understanding eSports Betting

Where there's competition, there's betting — eSports is no exception.

Betting in eSports works much the same way as it does in traditional sports, with minor tweaks to accommodate the unique characteristics of video games. There are several types of eSports betting: social betting, challenge betting, real money betting, skin and item betting, and fantasy eSports.

In social betting, individuals bet items or cash on the outcome of a game between friends. Challenge betting involves directly betting on the outcome of your game, pitting your skills against others with stakes involved.

Real money betting and skin/item betting are more traditional forms of gambling, where individuals place bets on the outcome of professional eSports matches, much like people would on a football or basketball game.

Finally, there is fantasy eSports, comparable to fantasy football, where you assemble a team of individual players and earn points based on their performance in real games.

9.3. Components of an eSports Bet

When you decide to engage in eSports betting, you'll likely be faced with several options depending on the platform you choose. Some common components of an eSports bet include the Money Line (predicting the outright winner), Handicap Betting (odd-makers will give advantages to the underdog to balance the market), and Total Betting (betting on the total number of points, games, kills, etc., in a match).

When it comes to betting on eSports, the most common type of bet is the Money Line Bet. But more experienced bettors might choose to engage in Handicap or Total Betting to increase their potential winnings or challenge themselves.

9.4. A Deep Dive into eSports Betting Markets

Different games offer different betting markets. For instance, in Counter-Strike: Global Offensive, viewers can bet on everything from the overall winner of a match to who will score the first kill. In contrast, in League of Legends, options range from the outright winner, to the team who slays the first dragon, to the player who scores the first kill.

Betting markets can also include 'futures' bets where bettors predict the winner of a tournament rather than a single match. Or 'proposition' bets where a specific event within a match would happen — such as the first player to die or the team to collect a certain object first.

9.5. Strategy and Tips for eSports Betting

As is the case with any form of betting, having a well-thought-out strategy can significantly enhance your winning potential when betting on eSports.

One key strategy is understanding the game. Familiarize yourself with the rules, gameplay mechanics, and key strategies employed by teams. Understand which matches are important and which are not – team motivation is as important in eSports as in any other sport when it comes to predicting outcomes.

Further, be sure to stay informed about the eSports scene you're betting on. Knowing about team form, player changes, recent results, and head-to-head records can give you a competitive edge when placing bets.

9.6. Fantasy eSports Leagues

Fantasy eSports leagues are a different beast altogether. Unlike traditional betting, they pose less risk, as they're often free to enter — although some paid leagues offer higher rewards.

In fantasy eSports, you assemble a virtual team of real players and earn points based on those players' performances in real matches. This adds an entirely new dimension to watching eSports, making even less important matches exciting as the performance of individual players can drastically affect your fantasy team.

Competing in fantasy leagues requires a deep understanding of the game and its players, as well as strategic thinking to balance your team within the given budget. There are various platforms online where you can join leagues and compete against players globally.

In conclusion, eSports betting and fantasy leagues offer an exciting and engaging opportunity for fans to become more involved in the eSports world. Whether you're betting on the outcome of CS:GO matches, or carefully curating your fantasy League of Legends team, it provides a thrilling way to engage with eSports beyond just observing. With careful strategy and understanding, it also offers an exciting potential avenue for wealth-building. So why not give it a try and immerse yourself in this fast-paced, heart-pounding world of eSports? It's game on!

Chapter 10. Navigating the Legal and Regulatory Challenges of eSports

Online gaming, despite its boom over the past two decades, remains a heavily unregulated industry, both domestically and internationally. However, some recent legal developments are starting to shape the industry's landscape. This chapter delves into some of the significant legal challenges and regulatory complexities that investors and gamers must navigate in order to successfully capitalize on eSports opportunities.

10.1. Understanding the Legal Landscape

The first step in successfully navigating the legal landscape is understanding the parties involved in eSports: the game developers/publishers, league organizers, team owners, players, and fans. Each party has its unique legal considerations, which often overlap and intertwine in complex ways.

For instance, game developers and publishers control the intellectual property rights for each game. Thus, they play a significant role in issuing licenses for organizing eSports tournaments and streaming gameplay online. Violations of these rights can lead to legal disputes and hefty fines.

League organizers have to deal with employment laws to determine whether players are employees or independent contractors. They must also navigate gaming laws, which vary by jurisdiction, to determine where they can legally operate and host events.

Team owners face similar employment law challenges regarding player contracts, immigration laws for international players, and even child labor laws for minor players. Players must ensure their contracts are fair and lawful, while fans have to navigate privacy laws when streaming content or making purchases.

10.2. Overcoming Regulatory Challenges

Despite the rapid growth of eSports, many legal issues remain unregulated, leaving players, team owners, and investors vulnerable. The absence of a governing body that can set and enforce standards across the industry is a significant challenge.

Contrary to conventional sports, eSports lacks structures like player unions, agent licensing programs, and standardized contracts. This lack of structure results in inconsistent and often exploitative contracts, where players may not fully understand the terms of their employment.

Furthermore, the issue of player rights carries significant weight. Players, especially minors, often work under strenuous conditions with extended hours of practice and competition. Establishing guidelines and minimum standards for player rights and working conditions is paramount for the industry's sustainability.

10.3. Tackling Gambling and Betting Regulations

One significant regulatory challenge for eSports is the legal status of betting on eSports competitions. It falls into a regulatory gray area because it is not explicitly addressed in many jurisdictions' laws. This can be a critical consideration for investors, who may want to invest in companies that operate eSports betting platforms.

These platforms must navigate complex and often contradictory laws across national and state boundaries. While some jurisdictions have started to write legislation specifically addressing eSports betting, others continue to operate under laws written for traditional sports.

Additionally, the prevalence of "loot boxes" and other forms of in-game purchases, commonly considered a form of gambling, is another controversial issue. Governments worldwide are grappling with the regulation of such practices, leading to a legal environment mired in uncertainty.

10.4. Legal Issues Surrounding Streaming and Broadcasting

Technological advances have made eSports a global phenomenon, with matches streamed live via various online platforms to millions of viewers worldwide. However, the global reach of streaming platforms generates a complex web of legal issues, especially where copyright law is concerned.

Gameplay streams rely heavily on copyrighted content like the game itself, the players' characters, and often music or other types of copyrighted content. Moreover, different jurisdictions have vastly different copyright laws, making it nearly impossible to comply with all different rules and regulations.

Navigating the legalities that surround eSports is clearly a complex task. Whether you're an aspiring player, a potential team owner, an organizer, a developer, or an investor, understanding these landscapes is crucial. As eSports continues to grow at an explosive rate, we can likely expect further development, clarification, and standardization of its regulations across the globe. That is why, in this current climate, it is vital to stay informed, adaptable, and always consult with qualified legal counsel in your eSports endeavors.

Chapter 11. eSports: The Future of Entertainment and Wealth Building

The eSports industry, once a subset of the video gaming industry and dismissed as a novelty niche, has rapidly grown into a multi-billion dollar behemoth, capturing the attention of audiences and investors worldwide. Fueled by technologies like streaming services, digital platforms, and high speed internet, along with the ever-growing popularity of video games, eSports now represents the embodiment of entertainment's future and a completely new domain for wealth building.

11.1. The Winds of Change in Entertainment

Modern eSports as we know it began to take shape in the early 2010s, but it wasn't until the latter part of the decade that it really took off. This growth was largely fueled by several key trends. First, the global increase of high-speed internet access made online gaming accessible to a larger population. Second, the popularity of streaming services, such as Twitch and YouTube, allowed players to broadcast their gameplay to millions, spawning a new form of spectator sport. Finally, the surge in smartphone and tablet usage further broadened the pool of potential gamers and spectators.

Notably, the appeal of eSports isn't just about the games themselves but also the vibrant communities they foster. Platforms such as Twitch offer interactive experiences where viewers don't just passively consume content but engage directly with streamers and other viewers, blending elements of social media and traditional entertainment.

11.2. eSports: An Investment Paradise

Just as television catalyzed the growth of conventional sports, videos, live streaming, and advanced internet infrastructure have made professional gaming a lucrative, investment-worthy industry. Global eSports revenues have skyrocketed from $194 million in 2014 to an estimated $1.1 billion in 2021, according to Newzoo, a games market insights and analytics company. This impressive growth has drawn attention from from high profile investors, advertisers, and endorsements, marking a significant milestone in the legitimization of eSports as an industry.

Investors can get involved directly by investing in teams and tournaments, directly funding leagues, or sealing sponsorship deals. Indirect avenues include buying shares in game publishers or equipment manufacturers, or investing in companies that provide essential infrastructures like streaming platforms or high-speed internet services.

11.3. The New Goldmine: eSports Teams and Players

It was not long ago that being a professional gamer was inconceivable. But today, top eSports players earn six- and seven-figure incomes. Additionally, the valuation of individual teams has shot up as investors, looking for opportunities, have begun to pour funds into player contracts, facilities, and support staff.

Indeed, one of the most direct ways to get involved in eSports as an investor is by investing in a team. Early investments in these teams were made by wealthy individuals with a personal interest in gaming. However, as the value and earnings potential of these teams has become clearer, institutional investors and mainstream corporations have also started to get involved.

Some of the biggest eSports organizations, such as Cloud9, Team SoloMid, and Liquid, now have valuations well over $400 million with major investment from celebrities and traditional sports veterans who see a ripe opportunity.

11.4. The Indirect Yet Lucrative path: Game Developers & Equipment Manufacturers

Game developers are the lifeblood of eSports, creating the games that make the tournaments possible. Major players like Activision Blizzard, Riot Games, and Epic Games have founded multiple successful eSports franchises, and the success of these franchises directly impacts their bottom line. Moreover, these developers also take a share from in-game purchases or licensed merchandise.

A less obvious but equally lucrative path for investors is companies producing gaming equipment. With eSports athletes and fans demanding the best equipment, companies that manufacture specialized gaming mice, keyboards, high-resolution monitors, and ultra-fast GPUs are enjoying huge sales boosts due to the eSports boom. Investing in these companies could be another way to indirectly profit from eSports.

11.5. The Sky-High Potential of the eSports Market

As eSports keeps pioneering the digital age, it will continue to blur the boundaries between entertainment, sport, and social interaction. Unlike traditional sports, eSports has the advantage of being relatively immune to physical-world disruptions, as demonstrated during the COVID-19 pandemic when other sports came to a standstill but eSports continued to thrive.

Further, the local physical boundaries that apply to traditional sports do not apply to eSports. Tournaments can draw competitors and spectators from all corners of the globe, with matches watched by millions of dedicated fans. This international scale offers vast untapped potential for growth that no industry has had the privilege of harnessing before.

In conclusion, the transformative nature of eSports, paired with its adaptable and global reach, offers a treasure trove of opportunities for creators, consumers, and above all, investors. The industry is poised for explosive growth over the next decade. By staking a claim in this dynamic market now, investors could secure a piece of a potentially multi-billion dollar future. Accompanied by the right knowledge, foresight, and strategic action, eSports, indeed, presents an exciting, compelling, and promising frontier for investment.